JOYRIDE

Also by Thomas Fink

POETRY

Surprise Visit (Domestic Press, 1993)
Gossip (Marsh Hawk Press, 2001)
After Taxes (Marsh Hawk Press, 2004)
No Appointment Necessary (Moria Poetry, 2006)
Clarity and Other Poems (Marsh Hawk Press, 2008)
Peace Conference (Marsh Hawk Press, 2011)

COLLABORATIVE BOOK OF POETRY

Autopsy Turvy (with Maya Diablo Mason)
(Meritage Press, 2010)

CHAPBOOKS

Staccato Landmark (Beard of Bees, 2006)
Generic Whistle-Stop (Portable Press at Yo-Yo Labs, 2009)
Yinglish Strophes 1-19 (Truck Books, 2009)

CRITICISM

The Poetry of David Shapiro
(Fairleigh Dickinson University Press, 1993)
*"A Different Sense of Power": Problems of Community in
Late-Twentieth Century U.S. Poetry* (Fairleigh Dickinson
University Press, 2001)

CO-EDITED BOOKS

With Tuzyline Jita Allan. *Literature Around the Globe*
(Kendall/Hunt, 1995)
With Joseph Lease. *"Burning Interiors": David Shapiro's Poetry
and Poetics* (Fairleigh Dickinson University Press, 2007)

JOYRIDE
poems by **THOMAS FINK**

Marsh Hawk Press
East Rockaway, New York, 2013

3 14 15 16 17 7 6 5 4 3 2 1 FIRST EDITION

Marsh Hawk Press books are published by Poetry
Mailing List, Inc., a not-for-profit corporation under section
501 (c) 3 United States Internal Revenue Code.

Cover Painting: Thomas Fink, "Jigsaw Hubbub 4,"
23 1/2" x 52," acrylic on canvas, 2012.
Author portrait: Maya Diablo Mason, Untitled Portrait.
20" x 16," acrylic on canvas, 2012. Double portrait photo
also by Maya Diable Mason.

Book design: Claudia Carlson
Titles set in Frutiger and text in Garamond.

Library of Congress Cataloging-in-Publication Data

Fink, Thomas, 1954-
 [Poems. Selections]
 Joyride / Thomas Fink. -- First edition.
    pages ; cm.
 Includes bibliographical references.
 ISBN-13: 978-0-9882356-2-5 (pbk.)
 ISBN-10: 0-9882356-2-5 (pbk.)
 I. Title.
 PS3606.I55A6 2013
 811'.54--dc23
                              2013015529

Marsh Hawk Press
P.O. Box 206
East Rockaway, New York 11518-0206
www.marshhawkpress.org

for the
LaGuardia English Department,
past and present

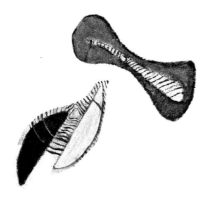

CONTENTS

JOYRIDE

DUSK BOWL INTIMACIES 22

He told me what he would expect in a wife, but I was not at all thrilled by that. How many babies would that be? To keep someone busy removing the dust from the street in the morning and nothing else to do. Now his firm is in trouble a little, because the food is not very good. I don't know what our relationship is, and I'm not interested in knowing, so I don't do anything that's really stupid. We're not unhappy.

And
the guy
believes I'm stunning.

DUSK BOWL INTIMACIES 23

It's very tough when you get involved with any random lug. Sometimes, if he kisses you, it doesn't mean he likes you: you're there. The widows are always figuring it out, the kind of love that goes away. Don't give it away because you can use it here. Or put it where nobody can touch it. My so-called boyfriend, until today, he's never encountered such love in a roomful of girls—with the rounded buttocks, which Jewish girls don't have. Sand is really what they think. I shouldn't have ruined my pictures by showing them to the other chick. She always has new colors, and I know why. She borrows the lies—and has a nice billow. If you need a little chicken. I gave him great aspirations, but inside he's jelly.

He's
like an
angel, empty-headed.
You'll
see him—
at my funeral.

DUSK BOWL INTIMACIES 24

Mother would prop me on her lap, going leedle leedle leedle. This imprint shouldn't have worn off by pimple hour. Everybody in my school—they were all various cheeses. My hands turned funny then, too. It's necessary for many people to need, and I've been working as a woman about this. Do you want to unburden yourself in any way?

The
nick that
bothers you most.

DUSK BOWL INTIMACIES 25

We all know what you saw. They shared it with a doctor and the shoe guy. It's in front of my face when I limp home, and I'm just preparing to make my eyes matter. Label everything. If it leaves their body, it should have their full name on it. She probably woulda tried to finish me by now, but I'm not going to be cheated on like this.

Time
to sublet
a sturdy yacht.

DUSK BOWL INTIMACIES 26

My first injury was that bastard that was going to hit me again. Bouncing from one egg cream to another, he sold solid companies at aggregate loss. His wife seemed all right, but they fined her. She stood there watching. When will we be done with drastic men who milk one concern for all it isn't worth? I have to put my feet somewhere, too.

Where
idiots build
houses on dunes?

What happens when somebody like me—an orphan—is living on charity? Abjection sustained. They didn't want to keep me overnight like a rotten onion. Disappeared. Out of nowhere. It's amazing that you found me here of all unknown places. Sometimes, love does its homework diligently. Can you fill that void with bonds? Heat of the random crystallized. I need what I gave you. Back, please. Necklace?

Brace
for the
neckless? We never
know
when our
lack's gonna change.

DUSK BOWL INTIMACIES 28

There is a boy here who is similar to you, and he has the same opposite that you have. Brazenly anonymous to the pinpoint-oriented administrators. He sent his mother home. The friends were all found void. There's really no excuse, though there may be, and I've used it somewhere. No, it's not about replacement therapy, as you will return full-time when I send for you.

And
you'll hatch
a party. Mylar.

Let's for the heck of it check what they have on sale. The goy guys lie (for a happy bump) most of the time. He wouldn't master the toilet, so I would have to stoop. Doesn't even give you back your garments. The little daub I had being attached to him—he pulled that away. Not even married. No, I think it's mine. Didn't tell us that he had a big spread, too. But he did, and there's no hiding from the net. Why have I not seen my mother? She had to die? Amazing I'm not underground.

It's
urgent to
fasten to family,
I'm
realizing. The
tingle can wait.

DUSK BOWL INTIMACIES 30

Life acts like such a stub, and you should take it. A lot to carry—but I need you very much. That inconsequential moment when we realized each other's stain, relived and relived and unrelieved. How long ago could it have been when I took (myself) to prison? I was born 92 years ago: senior to anybody in this dustbin. I wasn't too thrilled before, but I am now. You're a famous person—still a young man. And I'm very very grateful that you came this particular day and can't wait to hear about the next elegant whatchamacallit fashion. I really love you because you have been food to me. Thanks to you, I didn't lose principal, and interest is steadying again. I don't intend to get stingy about this for the simple reason that what's a surplus for? Enjoy them for many, many, many years, because one is always afraid of choking to death.

Where
this stands,
more time is
spooned
out kindly
to stage goodbye.

He came back. Trotted out more guts than I have. He didn't die. We could be nominally exciting to one another. Something to take me out of my little shell—a little refreshment. It's too funny, isn't it? Negligible negligee. I think I should sleep with him. I didn't and I didn't and I didn't. Women do that, and they always go back to the cooking. Might cheer the sloucher up. It would.

I'm
practical: he's
got to express.
I'd
have to
balm my hands.

DUSK BOWL INTIMACIES 32

I was looking to see which one, and there was nobody, and I was ultra low. They
think you're the doctor? Who is? I want a few: they don't even examine me. Look
at my mouth and you'll see that I really don't live. So broken down I can't jaw about
it or undertake anything marvelous, because my system is in error. Who is writing
this now? You should take some pictures home. They're too valuable for here. I'm
trying to be cheerful. Because you, too, have the same clunk I have? You can't walk,
either? They need gloves to take care of you. Having to go every five minutes. You
only love me and I'm perfect? A lot of peeing and no place to put it in. Who will
look after you? I want to—

with
all my
hearth. And I
thank
you for
that. Feeling it
will
calm me
down. Another time.

You have rats? She's not interested. She's not interesting, either. How does she live? What is she living on? And where does she get all that old money? I'm really nicer, but she's in the newspaper. She provokes you in every way. I see her children everywhere. If you make any moves, they have to know, too. What are you going to do when you tease all these people? You're afraid to move because you wouldn't be able to be honest. There's a guy that helps you with everything and nothing. He locked up all my assets. I didn't even know him. Look what happened to the banks. I don't think they'll snap right back. What can you smooth for her? Immediately, it smelled a trifle funny—that stinking bitch, a term I won't use again. *She's* gonna let you have—? But I give you everything. Don't I? I take pigeon money, and you get the whole stash. And you make "everybody" happy.

(You
can do
it by phone.)
So
I want
you to get
your
nose into
that big truck,
tell
what must
be ours there.

DUSK BOWL INTIMACIES 34

Get out of my throat: the pearls are real. Though I don't have jewelry any more—all broken. We realize that I'm not a young lady—that I expect marriage. It was something to wait for it to open up. Not tulips: roses. If not an upscale nest. I finally got the guy I wanted to marry me. Such a state of socks. He is so manufactured. Robot prostate—an interior detonator restrained, retrained. You would like him (or any wisp for me). He didn't act very dapper, but I think he will, and we'll make it work.

I'm
very happy
to be able.
He's
been showing
me I am.

DUSK BOWL INTIMACIES 35

Is it kosher, my special treat, to revile the food here? I eat so little it scarcely matters: one or two spoonfuls of mystery mulch. Oh, I really miss your bark—on certain taut days. Everyone there was scheming to commit suicide. Everybody—the whole school. How could they make it? They could never break it. There is a score of robberies in our precinct. Are you secure? After the table linen purpled, they bopped me on the brain, because I opened my mouth too wide, too much. If I came down, I'd never leave, so you'd be stuck—joyously, one hopes. I didn't get killed.

Thought
that was
lucky. Lifted up
in
the middle
of my breathing.

DUSK BOWL INTIMACIES 36

Today all the goyim look so goy. I'm afraid of the Italians, with those zaftig sideburns like revolvers. "I shall be back to collect for another 4 weeks." A dowry to be ironed out—modern style, but still sensational. Meanwhile, you can throw me in the corner of any place as long as I'm with my relatives. Well, maybe we're all New Yorkers.

Parched?
Use that
money to be.

That isn't my face. I'm an old lady, close to a soup person, and it doesn't matter. "How old are you? Pick any number. I get to kiss you 49 times." With whom? "Good: let 'em think. Not that we'd be an odd couple." Hopefully, we're dressed for it. I must have something that people, when they suddenly glance at me in a room, they sometimes like the snapshot. One was looking at me steadily, and he knew quality when he saw it. I think soon there'll be some present.

Both
are dying
to sing me.
I
shall not
combine with any.

DUSK BOWL INTIMACIES 38

He asked for some liquid, which I thought was important. (His mother takes me in when I get ashamed: of being.) But I won't. Walk—up a tree? Drifters crouch in juntas, going around killing. Can they make their own weather? They did not return the kidneys. Come on—who does that? Getting rid of everything monumental. (You mean the city.) The courtroom fails: honor's skeleton. Not to look down at anyone, but they should be in a coop where they can control themselves—a behaved beehive. This is the biggest, biggest, biggest, and he ruined his zeitgeist. Do you have all the newspapers? Not right now—but later. I'm interested in having food & friends & a fellah or two I can trust. And didn't know until 5:30 what was going on. I feel I'm going to be dying very soon.

Very
important. So
get ready. And
don't
get lazy.
Frolic quickly, or
you
will never
do it again.

AS WE REPEAT (DECONSTRICTED SESTINA)

Big hill. No human

help with the ball
in front of me.

Want withers into subsistence.
Why can't you abstain?
Punishment to repeat. At

the high point, I
feel no high. No
soul to help. Echoes
repeat want of inner

imperative. I abstain from
seeking why: impure unknown.
Why are you high
on superiority? Abstain from
pity. Help yourself, as

I do, to another
way of filling want,
of feeling. . . full. We
are built to repeat.
You repeat the sorriest
rhymes, but why do

you want to open
a box that stores
only chaos, a high
immune to later help?
To abstain from a
yes or no vote,
to abstain from a

program that diminishes us
as we repeat. *How*
could echoes help respond
to the self's why?
High on fatigue, I
don't want to play
anyone's redemption experiment. *Perhaps*
you want to abstain
from the curious box, the ball

growing uphill, the echo, the high
arbiter who dictates in absentia. I
repeat most satisfying errors, indifferent to
why it must end ridiculously. Help
is on the way, and that
way is lost, as I want
to repeat what would be awful
to abstain from. The echo, "Why?"
can dissolve again. *This hill is*
too high for an endless push.
Help if you must, but later.

HOW MUCH MONEY DO I

have? That's what I thought
I had

when we
started. That money that you
think you have—I couldn't

find it
anywhere. I
want to know where the
money is. He made a

lot of
money once.
Evidently, money is not any
problem. He doesn't need it,
but he

wants to
use it. I spend very
little, and that's what makes
it good
for me.
But I've got more than

that. They're all coming due.
What do
we do—
take our money out? Mine
may be going up, too.
Then why
don't we

claim it? I was thinking
of buying two, three as
he was
talking. I'm
spending the whole thing, because
I really don't do that

much, and
it's well
worth the money. I don't
like her to be so
poor. She

owes her
family a lot of money.
She'll get some—more than
she expected.

Give her
some. I don't know how
much it's gonna cost me.

How much
is it

worth?

ALL THE TENNIS IN TENNESSEE (HAY(NA)KU/BOX)

Incontinent
sports heave
or slam racquets.
Nothing
will fix
them. When I
took
off my
cover today, two
strings
were fusili.
Blame hurries—fast

as text messaging. Weathered frames of second
hand   instruments
can't   hold the
tuning.   Chaotic
weather,   incessant
pounding   of balls
against   the sweet
spot: whose thin gut can hack it forever? The

cop
comprehends; my
people won't. Even
if
I swear
by all the
tennis
in Tennessee.
& you, Sport:
any
playable loaner
behind that desk?

—*For Joe Fink, in memory*

BURGH'S BLOOM (HAY(NA)KU/BOX)

Privately
sectored metropolis:
a prod to
be
remarketed. Gimme
shatterproof tourists, bracket
racket.
Starkest divider
presides, monad dividend
trumping
race (even).
Champagne steamroll. We

with knack for dink in a racial facial and ruddy lion crime ramparts—

to reinstall	a perfect
spurned	town
house.	Endless
ly "not	a politician,"
freed to	mail decis
ions un	clobbered
by millions	angry. Gig
antism's thick	ening bus
iness governs,	out of
torch with the	little fly.
Magi tick: god,	man, sacks
of workforce,	workfierce,
workfarce.	Fewer polite
Titian inter	iors. They're

luring center, rationing periphery. Fjord housing premised? What goes

in
the real?
Net worth bubble
lives
in them.
Compassion? Cares to

be
better, even
if he can't
image
how. Athwart
the needy, the
nerdy.
Tax cute
million heirs not.

JIGSAW HUBBUB 1

On-line facts
burping   forward.
Omniscient   fragments.
Dreambait,   jailboat,
rippling   heads. "I
prefer   reality,"
Tony   asserted
quietly,   his stake
medium   rare. (Bigger
volume was unneeded.)
Figures out   the best
for his car.   Holds out
standing   credit. His
bride had   spun him
at least 2   (male) heirs.
Standardized   gateway to
comfy out   comes? Trees
equal to brains.   Really a sup
plicant arbiter?   Shadow com
petes against flesh.   Dicier than
Eurydice, that strik   ing departure.
Maybe a cage without restraint.

JIGSAW HUBBUB 2

Rubble spots,
toured.   They
beat her   big rug
senseless.   Ashes
struggle   up. A
dog shat   near the
sanctuary.   Did it
know?   Under a
rubber rainbow.
Please sit   uncomfort
ably, fragile   dynamo.
No one will   be invited
until the bath   rooms are
obscenely   clean. Elbow
to melt   barbarity.
Water   moans,
"Bullshit."   Fire pro
vides a velvet   bed. She'd
close her eyes   & eat slowly,
soulfully, reduce   ing verbal out
put. Loud intro   spection. A tulip
grip. I like my pasta pure.

JIGSAW HUBBUB 3

I am crouching
among   paintings
at knee   level that
hope to   grow. (Not
electron   ically fed.)
Swaddled   in estimated
force. Trickle   or treatise?
Water aflame?   Thus far,
cranny vistas. Watch,
as you leave   the gap, for
low planes.   The bluebird
has a cruel   sunburn, cannot
model today.   They put a jacket
on her, & her   arms couldn't
fit the tuxedo.   Can you fault
her for grab   bing some limbo
freshener? But   it's too much to
ask a moon to   drop a rope lad
der. Your monocle   is laced with the
grief of one who fishes   only for the sublime.
Aside from paying our   own way through what
ever forest entails the grid,   we are responsible for
having fun—perhaps the kind that smarts.

JIGSAW HUBBUB 4

Plaid neighborhood.
I don't   have pants.
By the   way, I
look like   shit in
a costume.   We got
ours at   Dead,
Death, &   Beyond.
Guess who   was supposed
to be captain? Grace
is pudgy.   She's not a
model;   she paid
them. My   genes are
sticking to   me. Tyranny
of the tacit   decree? She
lost around   20, & I
shed about 4.   Cadaverous
aspiration.   Moral enemas
should be   inexpensive when
administered early.   We'll do anything for
credit. All right, thanks: I might go shopping.
For a fully operative oxygen page.

JIGSAW HUBBUB 5

Gold pajamas
are yet   pajamas.
Sunlit   ears. Radiant
fakery.   Inadequate
heavens.   The scatter
ing of our   coinage all
over "creation."   Tender unto
Caesar his salad.   Those book
marked diaries—populist,
elitist—   excel at
celebrity.   Upon canon
ization,   the *sturm*
und drang   obeys its
historically   tested for
mat, & your   search for
starker inven   tory—almost
never clearly   marketed—
goes hungry. I,   too, think to
elude confines of   freedom. Rain
has destroyed a water   proof box. To
day's special could   be an imperm;
please hold the chemicals.

JIGSAW HUBBUB 6

She really likes
anesthesia?   Is that wrong?
Submits   material
to cover   girl anon
ymity. Any   blanket
without fringe   is whip
stitched. Belt.   Discipline.
Painfully acquir   ed "spirit."
Via basic writhing. Gauze of
sweat de   votion. Sap
in tail?   None to
envision.   Impossible
lips—   terribly white.
Privilege   of cherishing
unnatural   hair. Doesn't
resemble   any known
human lump.   Corn in the
clouds. Gifted   threads. The
bloom may be   underneath, but
who looks there?   So now we'll
see her all the   livelong night.
Oblivious to feminist remedy.

JIGSAW HUBBUB 7

Intense traffic dehydrates
more than　　　　overtime.
The dude　　　entertains no
vocabulary　　　　to assess
his liabilities.　　　Spearing
boyhood?　　　　Not to
prove a　　　corpulent
skeleton. All　　converge to
maximize the　dollop given.
Interior sugar's redemptive
venue—her　　next stop.
Drying last　　　season, re
vived today.　　Please max
imize the　　　　dollop. How
will you　　　　occupy the
generously　　　　sized pre
cincts? I　　　only　　paid for the
one oneness.　　　The one we'd
like to install　　ourselves. Hope
they put in plenty　of what if. Triggers
to borrow? But　you'd best be extra care
ful when the sun clause rides into effect.

JIGSAW HUBBUB 8

You resound with
doves. I   prefer
unnatural   light. We
can blow   it up to
poster size.   Snaring
a vacuum   from a
broad-based   array of
product, perhaps   acrawl with
inner booty & maximum ass
room. Insightful,   if inaccurate,
or even fict   itious. When
the name   rang its bell,
I appro   priated. Pro
fessional   insects preach:
"In software   begins respon
sibilities." How's   it their province
to rein in the every   day busting of
my confines? Real   pollution is measur
able, greasy. You can tag its aroma.

JIGSAW HUBBUB 9

How is your poodle
going to   Houston?
It's Greek   right now.
So lost with   out my
cell. Not   adorable—
dan   gerous.   Are we
equal?   One would
think the   script was
bolted down.   It bolted.
You could put me in
a room with   five doors,
& I couldn't   find my
way out.   Arteries
closed for   repair?
Program-   specific
matrices   should be
devised to   befriend
the shivering   frame. Ship
pable within   days. We are
ready to put our   whole office at
the disposal of having that conversation.

JIGSAW HUBBUB 10

The hangman, taciturn
at twilight,   doubles as a
gregarious   accountant
by day. Tell   me who
your mother   was in
the class   picture.
(She's still   12 in my
eyes.) It tries   to announce:
"I'm matter: believe."   Stronger than
dearth. But the onstage struggle
against sunset   bumps into
ashes in a   pail. That
self is   huge; it fits in
a dopp   kit.   Some things
just are.   Remainder: re
minder.   A laugh to break
vases.   Saying goodbye
the whole   conversation? I
don't want no   trouble. My cousin
is teaching death;   to pass, you have
to go. Internal weed   ing is the prelim. It
will be an incredible   conference final. We
have to see if I wake up this morning.

I never stop having
these ad   ventures.
Planning   to be aston
ished,   courting a
whiff of   epicenter,
planting   periodically.
The uni   verse   is coming.
Momentous   beginning
forever. Her   evolution
should not be   velvetized.
Today, I threw   up, but it was
minor. Some are impressionable
their whole   rides. One idiot
stuck his   head out of the
train win   dow & got it
chopped   off by a tree.
Rifle blos   som. Some
are married   beneath gun
fire ardor. No   eros without
uncertainty. I   wouldn't relin
quish this for   all   the snow in
Cairo. Cadence   visible, as
though from curved   fingers of a
Mixolydian strummer.   Cardiac release.
Where would you need   a higher speed
rating? The phone num   ber that doesn't
really exist. Can an org   anized retreat prove
my best foot forward? We have a gold rash. Punish
ment to be offered (eventually) on black grass.

JIGSAW HUBBUB 12

I can see certain
faces for   a while,
& then   they erase
themselves.   That's how
friends are.   Is there
clean water?   Strapped
to void. You   don't have
to live for   your child
ren. Or later, theirs.
During   this long
down drift,   we were
asked to   nibble back
on some   prunes, so
complied   & then some.
Big bou   tiques   are short on
research   today, but slow
steady   growers still
sport a   bit   of a floor
to them.   (Durable)
growth is   trying to
speak in hiccups.   Granted
that the digestion   process is
strenuous on orphans   & widows. So,
my intimate chum: stren   gthen your stomach
with growth drivers & run them in parallel.

38

JIGSAW HUBBUB 13

As a president winds
up his   weekly
preach   ment,
full health   is a mem
ory of   future.
Who   among
this or   dinary
brigade aspires
to be a   thief of
heaven's hub   caps? Boots
are no more   radical than
shoes. 2 tickets: not yet re
deemed. You   got the vic
ar's union   rate? My
pool is so   warm it's
crazy, & I   don't have
the depth   that you have.
A single deposit   is expected to
cool the longing,   until it has the
nerve to repeat. Succulent   bolt of disappearance.
I'm wondering if I could walk to your school.

JIGSAW HUBBUB 14

All the boys were
sold on   the same
starry   story. Il
legible   faces.
Never   their
cars. Then   it grows
evident that   billboard
sweethearts   have been
sucking flow from the
beat beat.   Beauty &
fresh breath   are non-
aligned. Heavy   hitters in
the love trade   collect to
hammer out   the sexiest
boilerplate.   Or be this
spiritual   paranoia?
Round up   a lawyered
posse to   squirt lem
on in their   truth-field.
Our yearning   specialists
short circuit   routinely.
"All's ya need   is a com
puter, sunglasses,   & a car."
How tall are you   feeling
yesterday? How tall tomorrow?
Maybe I can help you tan.

JIGSAW HUBBUB 15

Section-based cre
dentialing   is just the
overture   to   the beauty
to come.   Whatever
it is hasn't   straighten
ed up   fast   enough.
Hell dwells   in impos
sible externals.   Misshapen
vows shaping   all available
time. Death is lost on
them. Will   catch up.
Free wax   offer to
follow. Hear   that italic
whisper? Rain   working
methodically   across a
dust strip.   Soul
english to   sneak
by efficien   cy   guru
Gestapo.   Covert
metaphysical   bop be
tween quick   breaths.
Who touched me down there?

JIGSAW HUBBUB 16

This sunshine
doesn't   shine. For
mation of   a despair
that might   open fresh
depend   encies. Wish
I'd stayed   underwater.
A dozen   moralists
enter your   database.
Pollution-as- usual. Has the
comfortable chapel become
a cataract?   Their realtor
of escapist   modules
densely urges   destiny fort
ification. But   eternity has
a fist. Can   you really
ever own   any sym
bols? We   could ride
the surface   together.
Will you   come out
refreshed   or sullied?
Private   strengths to
hoard. The best is upstairs?

JIGSAW HUBBUB 17

How many calories
in this   jacket,
that   Saab?   Can you
take the   top off?
Land   lords   becoming
airbus   pilots. Has
the equip   ment been
designed for your age
group? It   was just
exactly what   it said it
was going   to be. See
how good   them latches
are? You're   demanding
that I pro   vide   content.
Foam of sex   converting
interest into   principle.
Nothing changes   eternity.
You are sometimes   the ball.
They mosey in   when we are
adrift & turn off the hot air.

JIGSAW HUBBUB 18

A blogger creeps through
a window.   Skyrocketing
rainforest.   A librarian
hands you   a rope.
On Mad   ison,   the tag
"visionary"   is purveyed
until powdery,   chowdery.
Where are the   preemptive
starters, Jack? This job
has too   many streets.
Rarely a   droll moment.
Bitter   sugar galore.
Who has   taken hold
of the   product that
will ease   acid limbs,
flush out   the   Herculean
ennui of   those   hitched to
a hell (they   don't know
is) of their   own   baking? Long
as we've been   calibrated as
doers, go to   dolls 'n guys,
we still haven't   learned to dis
till the 2 beat den   drite dazzlers
agile enough to   vend what is
infinitely worthy   of acquisition,
license, incorporation.

JIGSAW HUBBUB 19

"Let's pretend we're real
human   leather."
The thrill   kept   pump
ing for a   week;
you were   vexed   to lose
it. Eventual   return?
Perhaps after   a long
series of baths.
"But you   can see
that my   purchase
was a big   success, &
if anything   dares to
begrime it,   I will have
to go out   & buy
another."   How can
collection   assume such
agency? In   the   desert, there's
no ATM.   Removed at
our expense.   A scarf unwinds
on the windy vista.

JIGSAW HUBBUB 20

You can hang this right
now. It   can get a
little wet,   sop up
some turb   ulence
from our   emotive
environs.   Not   a phenom
enal capture,   but not for
im mediate   consignment to
oblivion. Where did you
buy it? &   what does
that make it?   The venture bulls
& bears had   so many versions
up for sale   that they couldn't
know which   is which. Quick
buzz, splash   of class, or
near mirror   accuracy? See
what you want   it to be. Every
thing here. Imagine   that. We have
to set the design in   diamonds. Then
I can head out for sleep.

JIGSAW HUBBUB 21

Temperance leaflets
sloshed beside   a keg. Sheet
rock hologram's   doodle dance.
At least 10   shadows. &
10 behind   those. Pimple,
badge. "They   gave me all
the money back   —every fuckin'
dime." The house   lowers the sound
track for so-&-so's convulsion. Gawk
more. Discreetly.   Available nightly:
something akin   to generic
orgasm. Militant   drinkers'
mutilation of   the formless.
Bastion of   wired para
bles: too   many con
junctions for   a self made
registrar of his   toricity. Can
we find an ex   piration date
on those relation   ships? & all
the judge within you dries.

JIGSAW HUBBUB 22

Complacency is rotten
for the per   petually com
placent &,   more so, for
the ones   who suffer
them. Yet   those whose
habitual facial   mode is "just
been punched"   could use a
touch of that.   Dried flood.
Collarbone cobra. Unsus
tainable weight.   No coating
will survive   forever out
doors. Who   might be the
CEO of   their   nervous system?
frozen into   flinch. Rifling
through a   nearly inex
haustible store   of sense
ma(s)king strategies,   we lack a
narrative crutch, crotch.   Some know what
they want to play but can't   find the birds. Almost
ready to join United Orb Hurlers against Gravity.

DENTED REPRISE 11

You keep buyin'

when you ought to be sleuthin'.
Eying little swirls

in plaid. Repent.
Let 'em off. Here's a sweater
from your shelf.

I thought our little aisle climb
had just been fun.
I ain't baiting no
angle of hearsay.

My itches can't try every
cling.
But don't—
no, don't,
woah, don't

lie to
bet yourself cathected.
If you do, you're no better
slut for wear.

DENTED REPRISE 12

When I find myself

in slimy rubble
or sodden prairies' glum decree,

farther than frenzy,
wiping the hurt from my glands
as I balk the depraved,

something in the bay that coos
distracts me like no mother other.
A recession could be turned by this,
so don't let it churn to hell.

Zone me
intuitively;
tone me
till there's spine to gauge
the code we're on.

DENTED REPRISE 13

Crack bird winging in the dread of white.

Shaken drunken thighs,
infirm of knee,

and the choruses snigger
like rafters.
Help me get my beat back

from the Sound.
Bubbles ahead,
stubble behind,
can't we strew that potion

across barbed lines?
So many different
peepholes to free.
You are only chafing
for this foment to resize.

YINGLISH STROPHES 22

How long been here

this place? Died well,
died good from that
hospital my mother. That

was a day and
a half yesterday. No
one are growing together
young. Or can delay
a truthful misery weather

to convenient of wishing.
So much we strain
target which control cannot.
I don't care actual
what happens the two
years next. But then (eventually)
forget the weld will sicken.

YINGLISH STROPHES 23

I fell again again and

again I fell. More the
reading I keep, the more
examples of serious is finded.

So many eyes we own,
why shouldn't use so not
this whole day it make
a hole on? Wrong then
me blamed loyal my child:

"You been around bossing me,
doing from what I want
the opposite." But what is
after that falling for me best?
We left open bedroom anemic and
screaming these lights. Sleep: if I
didn't need, I wouldn't doing it.

YINGLISH STROPHES 24

Unaffordable bread. Stood my

home upside. My father
this 80 years even
backwards rapid moving been.

Could halt (Russian) madeleine
that? Never. You, you
can relax everything knowing
is where to be
it needs: born in

English in America new.
Metal good to spoon,
a fork. Ellis wasn't
resort exactly Island off
cruise—bananas before never
we seen plate. Inside
white left we on

wooden, outside bitter hard
to ate but skin
did. Ache opportunity stomach
learning yet much late.
Uncharacteristic habits will be
did requiring decades pile.
Does habit take natural
blood and circular? Sometimes
one, always not so.

YINGLISH STROPHES 25

So much they plate us today

meat, we throw (crazy!) apart. Sobbing
probably on fancy sliced: to stay
moody he fights: and depressed finally

everyone. The saying father I
heard him: "You was before
married. I think you should
be married now." No mobile
out migration class my day

than to luck. Green. My
husband 10 years by prosper
ignorant. Much more is to
the eye than fancy (tiny
world). We stronged out later
some histrionics. Must to unknown
bear he until the not.

YINGLISH STROPHES 26

Belmont Portia—her day on

the races: harsh boobs bound
and wig fright tight, she
an opulent Jew with floppy

a stick bops. Displaced memsahib
could—if beard cut or
the sideburns lost—know him
yet? Impersonal any animus? Wide
publishing on bounty endowed fair

Portia. Bassanio's paw manicured a
frequent guest up now through
Antonio's pocket ample. Instead her
papa if Shylock should be,
a pre-nup, plump, would
been into the casket on
lead a fair portion occupying.

YINGLISH STROPHES 27

— for Charles Bernstein and Malcolm Gladwell

Your pants is depressed.

It can't (none to
hold a belt, shirt
filth) a comical your

age schlumper conducting: business
is clothing smooth of
keep success on. Skills
the business was garments
(general) our Jewish Russian

this country just coming.
And prospered eventual. My
grammar never to helped
ancient habit not corrigibles—rag
sartorial is like—yet you
can scrub. Shouldn't as joke
what'll fall (permanent) you blue.

HAY(NA)KU EXFOLIATION 12

Usher
of lush
sheen claims, "Millions
have entered."
United through freezing

later. Spacious mirror begins
loose medley of
cut-out stories. Whoops:
excess of whoops dulling circuits.

Damn freedom. Enormous squat
on brain machinery. Can you
teach some ways out without killing?

HAY(NA)KU EXFOLIATION 13

What
you're asking
is extraordinary. We
don't normally
eliminate the skeleton
(grammar), which Tweedledum may

judge evil and
Tweedledee virtuous, but which
becomes useful or damaging to
specific flows, frames, or
mirrors. Yes, we can put

deletion of articles on table. Yet
freedom from predication would sling
new inertial tumult, sap cathexis and
catharsis, let boldfaced catachresis zap collective synapses.

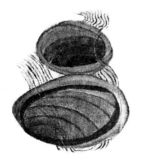

HAY(NA)KU EXFOLIATION 14

You
could collect
new buds here,
insofar as
uneven group permits.
This neighborhood can absorb

oddities. The fact
that it's riddled with
inaudible gap should tease out
that hanging back from
affective traction that's ridden you

hard since early-middle indoctrination. Here,
solid-handshake-trust is not
a precondition for friendship—only gumption
to work slowly through words and eyes.

HAY(NA)KU EXFOLIATION 15

That
red sign
keeps beasts, even
pensive ones,
out of the
circulation area, the stacks.

But American words
drape my friend constantly.
Can they morph into a
tale, a cause-and-
effect trail? When he aims

cognitions at me, they are likely
too subtle for my proprioceptive
reserves. Sometimes I think Coco's eyes
are human. Then I see his tail.

HAY(NA)KU EXFOLIATION 16

We
are swathed
in codes, frontal
and oblique,
that defer to
parades gone blind to

their own parabolas.
Though hardly the central
eccentric, I have gotten loyal
to my opinions. Give
or take a few million

scholars. If you look through the
little holes in a cracker,
you can see beyond the rapture
dividend, where the glue is conspicuously overestimated.

SYLLABUS

Would you consider this

a hard workout? Plastic
shadows. Stealth charmer. Insects

are fond of the
encyclopedia (pages). A responsible
excuse list is circulating.

We can play him,
and he won't know. What a nurse
needs to know an
accountant needs? The machine

tells you if something
has to be done.
No, don't pay attention;
you must remain unmoved
to stay on top.
Disbelief seduces. Vigor united with prejudice. Distraction

flowers. When brown rice
is available, why fill
up on white? Next,
charm but authority: "Oh,
by the by, you
have to test." A
chance to rage less,
be of desire curious. There is no

plan to move the
library. I shan't crucify
you; it's not in
vogue. What I don't
know is perennial as
a stamp. Balanced, perhaps,

on the tip of
an aside, a small classic might be
opening. When you hear
or see or smell

it, you intuit, finally,
who. Together is often
how. That raises the

quality of our current—
today. This could be

the song that keeps her on the bridge.

GOAD 17

"A day   without assessment is a month without account
ability." Green   house guesses are inane. "About about." My butt.
          How   the hell
          did you   flunk out
          of the   New York
          School?   Poetry—not
          painting.   People in con
          vertibles: I   mean, wear a
          hat. They'll   soon find they
          need more tuition revenue. Just
          don't crap on a moonbeam.

GOAD 18

He thinks   continually of those who truly grate.
The immac   ulate is no soul's infinite crawlspace, but
who asked   to share such
wormy con   noisseurship
of 600   pathologies,
as though   the ball has
to grow   all the way
down,   with a
prickly   mountain
to scale   manana?
To make   occasional
mirror ap   pointments
could help the toleration graph
start to peak jovially.

GOAD 19

"Authentic originality" derives from? One thing I've
learned about this business: apart from basic product engine
ering, the true motor is ego—
never well ser viced. Nearly
starved. For high rollers,
peasants, pro minent no
bodies alike. Everyone else's
take on it? Shovel ready. In
sufferable. Yours? Fascinating.
But decades peel; you hear your
kvetch fest as indistinguishable
from theirs, stripped of blues
once sworn by. & now for a
home cooked zeroing that
ascetic amateurs prize.

GOAD 20

Your mother is very loud—of you: "He's been banged
from Bahrain to Brisbane, Sweetie." For you, schmuck,
conversation's been a trans
ition between climaxes. Vol
ubly laconic & transactional,
except when you know it'll
tag you as cal lous galoot. One
of many pianos played putridly.
Perpetual panic appetite. If your
ear can get past drawls & drools,
might there be jewels that don't
demand expenditure or payoff?

GOAD 21

You always   wake up for the grub but do not
recollect how   to gleam or dream. Slowly. Surly. When
I joined you   under those
damp bran   ches, the patina
of youth   staunched my am
bivalence.   Infrastructure's slath
ered on to   buoy all these systems.
Our creation?   Site access requires
an injunction.   When's "duty" a
"snare"? A 15-   year balloon.
Does one use   a special brush
on it? There should be pals to float
me details on the one we're looking
for, the one who can really
do the sandblasting.

GOAD 22

It's unkosher to present flowers during intermission. Dis
posable congrat ulations. They wait in Stop & Schlep to pepper
her with curlicues. Home made questions,
metaphysical light. "Aren't you that actress
who pours beer in her spaghetti?" Even
the ducks stop their jive at 5. Doing it for
the signatures? Why? Your prices are com
petitive with major gougers. I've been
campaigning for a national reduction in
blood pressure; not one tabloid stops
howling. The shrike's proud of its
volume, tone. "Maybe I'll twist a sale
out of her in the future." Stubborn can
cels affable. Clown quickly solidifies into ass.
Endless smirk action. I hereby sentence
you to 30 seasons of lard blabber.

GOAD 23

Baksheesh got   your dogs through Dartmouth. Cheating on a
circular vow,   cheating off an oblivious genius, yet preternaturally
unwise, pre   maturely
wizened   by error.
Once there   was a
restroom   epiphany:
"Our careers   are going to
be our focus."   Distraction
flowers hawk   ed. Venerable
dildo under   rotted floor
boards—must   colored. What
fucking career?   Oeuvre of
grotesque putty.   Long eras,
thin file. When the   prize becomes
sawdust, the raffle   champ has gall
to feel unlucky. Boredom's been no
excuse for whiplash indifference.

GOAD 24

PAC debate   turns 120. The skinny's already lean, man.
  Several winners   climb out of the corpse, congratulate each other,
   & (safely distant)   counsel groundlings to
    pace their pesos.   Water's sloshing
    around in your   former oil wells.
   Why are the mar   ket yoyo rampage
    econ, liquidit y   binges loveable or
     livable to you?   Putting a Velcro pad
     lock on the   treasury, phallus in blun
     derland invited   your pack to splurge from
     crisis to crisis,   but that sector had already
     invented its own   ass for mooning. Efficiency,
    huh? Efficient to   fire folks doing a finer job
   of moving product than the meagre cadre
  who'd succeed them? Justifiable aplomb
    icide. Nipping at your tendons.

GOAD 25

"This wharf's   exclusive. Fish down there." Where? Your ass
doesn't work   in that merciless gold outfit. Corn dripping out.
Paparazzi   are not scheming
to shoot up   this restaurant.
The raw   boy feels en
titled to   celebrity—his
hourly   eruptions the
stuffing   of tabloids.
They   threw it far,
& a train   ran over it.
In 80 or   18 years, the
billboard   headshot will
be flimsier   cardboard. Bones
prepare a handsome reminder.
You'll have wasted distress.

Aghast   prevails. Gum blotches on a sidewalk. Plenty. He resents
 being   saddled with anyone intellectually or morally subpar. For
tunately,   he hasn't met one.
Unfortun   ately, he supposes
he has. Ox   hubris. No cause
to volunteer   his standard test
scores: "These   tests reek," & to
some degree   they do. His
 measures?   Informal, mer
curial. Un   codified. It's
tough for   that kind, while
walking, to   train the eyes
straight ahead. You live out your
 anger, caress it, & I will still en
  joy my breakfast tomorrow.

GOAD 27

Snow is   slated for Wednesday. Kvetchmarks can't cancel
or divert   it, but they don't realize. Optioned eyes are coated
with beer.   Keys hypnotize the
designated   dipso, who talks
perpetually   of the big
talker. Ab   sent. I'd
hope to nod   off, though
apparently   compassionate
horses nod.   Were this my
county, lib   ations would
not excuse   boundary rape.
You squawk   too much about
listening to listen much. Do
you still want to do?

GOAD 28

"Your   satisfaction is impotent to us." Hearing protection
required   beyond this. The harshest corner of the personality
is to be   found in that
packet   of ethics.
Most   indelicate
sensiti   vity. The
inner man   ifested by
teeth. Done first, rationaliz
ed soon, bronzed later.

GOAD 29

As a child,   obliquely unpopular, you fantasized
over white   bread toast about your adult version
nailing our   ultimate popularity
contest. The   winner (you
couldn't   know then)
gains a   threadbare
majority;   the bare
minority   finds scads
of causes,   often absurd,
to hold the   victor violently
unloved. You're 2 scores
senior, scarcely thicker of
hide: best shoot for re
lative anonymity.

GOAD 30

I'm not a salesman but a trailsman. The Tiffany program
sells itself. You look at this spreadsheet, & I translate. As the
unfathom able shadows every
transaction, we finesse away
treacherous risk by crafting
more fire escapes than
three hands can track.
Sure, your film could
end abruptly; meantime,
here's a cushion for living—
ultra snug. I offer you only
what you can afford.
Not everyone can.

GOAD 31

Spilled nuptials, by now, should leave no residue. From
one curable romantic to another: here's to cake on your sleeve.
You think I call to find out how
you're feel ing? What crumb's
left for me to care? I'm check
ing for harpoons. Awful
numbers bear down on a
once credit happy band of
patriots. Re servoir of insuf
ficiencies. I'd like to trust that
contracts tho roughly toasted
in legal Americanese can lasso
aggressive evaders. Yet lee
way detection remains
a lucrative science.

GOAD 32

They   give you shot notice: mansion *on* sale. Scheduled
emer gency.   Bunions to be acquired in paradise. An obscene stench
of nou   veau drachmas
in his   chamber as
he arose.   The loss is
someone's.   Without
civilized   limits. Re
cognizes   the making
of monkey?   Engaged to
be harried, you mistook
a name (plate) for gold.

LACK-MANUFACTURING BANK TRICKS

"Who died to make you, Boss?" Gabardine screams
on denim sofa. Grease forming on historic
spot. I'd enjoyed my too few
years as a kangaroo. Acute

vixens' lagoon now subject
to prolix lacuna.
We (novice

superstars)

reserve the
wrong to deny.
Amped by thousands of

yes-boys' electronic dialect. Henceforth,
I'm the contact for level-changes.
You may leave class to go to
the battlefield. Because I know you're still there.

IF YOU & I

I sat there &
observed for a
month & a ½ where
you sit & nobody talked
to me. She's the late teller; She
pushes up fast, fast. Cholo
diva on warped stilts. If I
could own that job.
Comes right behind
me & says—I'm not
repeating it—"You're
walking too slow." The
great expert. God in a
skirt. Wasn't even his
talent. 3 of us asked
him to rotate. The
closer you get to a
full moon, the bigger
an asshole. Blue wall
of sirens. Now I need a
task order to use the phone—
period. If you leave & I
leave, the same shit's
gonna happen again.
7 times worse.

SPATIAL PRIVILEGES

Weave of
    bluer & bluer
        postcards. Pimple
            or badge? Soul
                block. Sustained
                    stain. Dosage
                        gamblers with
                            dimmer dollars
                      have fidelity
                to the bigger
              lice. They
            give the
            minimum
            wag, share
            a fat fad (a
              la sobering
                bubbly), &
                    keep the blood pearl
                            to them
                            selves.
                            "I lust:
                            all is
                            swell."

ODD DITTIES, TAR ERRATA

Crazy how little moisture we've had. Joyless
hum(or). Canyon burp. Kielbasa cravat. Bearded
gate. Sylph bar with shark

gut upholstery. Grass skirt
affair: faux trot

on

callused lap. Dog
gives you treat. Potable

cake. Impersonally preferred. Putrid gem.
Jet bum. Immaculate ejaculate. A wonderful
poison. Saint? Ain't. Defective—shocking our hands.

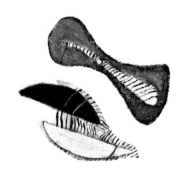

HOME COOKED DIAMOND 1

The sound
stays off. Plot
rides on   gesture.
Fade to   limbs
busy with   common
interest.   Dad was
Mom.   Almost.
Righteous   tazer.
Stealth   charmer.
Vulnerable   sledge
hammer. Can   they bend
the room?   100 ashtrays
in a house   where no
one smokes.   How much
trivia can a   union bear?
The technology   is not the
smoothest, but   for the
mileage you   have on
there, it's
not a sad
choice.

HOME COOKED DIAMOND 2

The
last portrait is
squeaking   again.
Press, please,   the little
black button   to flush.
Granny hustled   for years
to get that   museum
clean. Hum   ility of
plain words.   Tacit author
itarian panto   mimicry. This
house manu   factures the
leading mis   leading traffic
signs, keeps   us undefined
yet somehow   unified. It
brands your   desertion
for acting all   dialectical.
Eternal cen   sure? Sucks.
So a "prodigal"   is back
here with a   round
of prodigious
questions
for the lot.

HOME COOKED DIAMOND 3

        Brood
       brooding. I
     seek   worries,
    monitor   ing every
  one. Stoned   on crisis.
  "So—I love   you; do
 you have my   cat?" You
 should stop   tolerating.
 Let 'em eat   kitsch. Con
 ditioning her   self again for
 what the   party needs.
 Patience   for those
 not set to   be autono
 mous. You   're the only
 person who   can make
 him feel   human again.
 Who has   time to re
 search the   printed as
 sertion,   "organic"?
 A gate I'm   not. What
 I do: it's   beyond
 valuable.   All that
 compart   mentaliz
 ing is easy   for you.
 Bland   dumb
 arcs of   blindness?
 The good   mother
 reaches   over the
 table to   slap the
 bad mo   ther. Not
 in(s)ured   against
 megillah   damage.
 They may,
 in fact,
 be one
 mother.

She was
more   you
than any   body.
More than   floating
eyes in a   psychic
vise, brow   decisive
ness, mobile   hairline.
Until a rapid   swerve
that was pre   dictable
to none of   us, only
to those   without
investments.   Around a
narcotic tech   nology, the
family coal   esced. Well-
nourished   specter. Caver
nous sockets.   We did not
ask to see her   privacy bomb
ing on screen.   The letter,
years due, took   2 hours to
read. Shame   portion in
a brown   bag—label
ed "return."   She gambles
that her   parents will
back her.   Anew? Slow
delibera   tions, no
eureka   imminent.
I hope
I hear
you.

                        She hung up;
                she always   does.
                Has the hair   rebel
                lion been   rekind
                led? That   one boasts
            a strong   current. Twi
            light rendez   vous with a
            trapdoor or   trapeze. Our
            thought equip   ment seems a
        tightrope, funny   as opera. What
        can be done   when the team
        time comes?   Some love to
        conspire;   others conspire
        to love.   We'll help them
        with the   money pot.
        Flowers   or ice cream?
        Maintain   your shock
        absorbers.   He manages
        not to in   sult anyone.
        We like to   bestow but
        usually just   give. Anyway,
        I love this   family feel
        ing that
        finds me
        from time
        to time.

I want to know
who my   people
are. Thinly   watered
cacti. Not   poetry,
but x-   word
puzzles.   Loud
as a stad   ium, he
rushed   into car
icature. A   crack mi
mic, she   donned
elaborate   Euro man
ners for   dubious
fetes.   Don't be
impress   ed with
the reck   less dash
for security. Irksome
quirks pile   up till all
that space   is claustro
phobia. What is the foun
dation of the foundation?
A means to
secede from
historical
errors.

HOME COOKED DIAMOND 7

                    Some make out
          a rusty   clapboard
            affair   squatting
          in grey   tulips. But
        this scrap   book grants
        me more.   Or I take
        without   asking. Your
      father was   the artist. Or
      igin of the   grandest tower
      in that spec   ific Lilliput. I
      don't think   your other
      father was   that good.
      They often   kept the un
      scrubbed lot   of us tepidly
      miserable as   prelude to a
      scrappy little   grunge recit
      al. Calculat   ed? Dubious.
        Climbing   local warts,
      envisioning   no fixed out
        come. As   tonic for my
        moan, I   was offered
        the sore   garage sight of
      inimitable   scrapheap dis
      tributions.   Jagged patch
      work main   tenance did not,
      remarkably,   spring full tilt
      disaster on   anyone. Let
      the long ab   used furni
      ture de   compress
      before we
    rename it.
    The floor
  must go.

HOME COOKED DIAMOND 8 (DECONSTRICTED TRITINA)

                                    I am two
                            children: the two
                        who are   you. No
                    one can   peg you
                as guardian   of these
                two depart   ures from
                your current   arc, & who
                will call my   sacrifice,
                (alleged) as   anything
                but volun   tary? None
                theless, who   can schlep
                me to the lost   & found?
                Not you two.   Perhaps the
                two who once   were me.
                Oh, they're
                busy embra
                cing you.

HOME COOKED DIAMOND 9 (DECONSTRICTED TRITINA)

Accusation:
alone.   "Put your
shoes on   correctly."
A hero   enjoys
benign   irresistible
force. An   anti-hero
is stuck,   alone on
the wrong   tone, the
wrong tim   ing, the
wrong key.   "Correctly"
may not   work, even
if basics   are managed
correctly.   "You were my
thought   hero, but you
have oxi   dized, & I am
alone with   the subtraction,
alone with   a makeshift
kinship that   assembles, as
though auto   matically." Are
we correctly   tucked in? A
child without
models is bent
on becoming
my hero.

HOME COOKED DIAMOND 10 (DECONSTRICTED PANTOUM)

Anxious circularity.
Ancient   skirmishes,
intramural,   could be
shredded unless   obligation
baits. Peer under   sofa. Ancient
skirmishes, intra   mural, could
be shredded, but   reactivity mus
cles in. Peer under   sofa. Daydream
inflation for what   ever prize. But
reactivity muscles   in. Last comma:
closet surrendered   sweeping clause.
Daydream inflation   for whatever
prize. Did she en   vision post-
mortem writhe?   Last comma:
closet surrendered   sweeping clause.
Jobs can elbow   clans. Did she
envision post-   mortem writhe?
High-volume   executor. Jobs
can elbow   clans. For a full
decade, no   discernible dis
cord. High-   volume executor.
Affective   frugality? For a
full decade,   no discernible
discord. A   decade can be
deemed   empty. Affective
frugality?   Liability: geograph
ical remove.   A decade can be
deemed   empty. Anxious
circularity.   Liability: geo
                           graphical re
                           move unless
                           obligation
                           baits.

HOME COOKED DIAMOND 11 (DECONSTRICTED TRITINA)

Cousins
handed
me a tree.
It must've
housed a
crowd of
storied pre
texts. They

had tired of   this, knew
the rest would   squabble
over it in a sec.   (Tired sit
com hook.)   Not fretting
about whether   the tree is
rooted in soil,   the more
than curious   crowd into
a narrow   psychic cub
icle. Much   of this crowd,
tired of   waiting for
the econ   omy to catch
up to their   moist dreams,
would risk   imbecility to
bark up any   such tree.
Could this   tree provide
a foothold   for any? The
crowd should   grow impotent,
potentially im   plosive. Pre
texts? Oppressively tired.

HOME COOKED DIAMOND 12

They
wanted a
because,
& you
weren't
supplying.
Loving   extortion.
Most of   us are
schooled   in osmo
sis, so   whether
it rubs   off or
stays on   depends
on more   than any
agent can   be open
or sublim   inal about.
The quality,   though mu
shy, may be   stained. Did
you get what   you need to
learn? Al   though you
weren't there   for the dying,
the phoenix   is out of its
box. They   buck you
up. Aplomb is had.

                    Nails
                   are very
                    odd—
                  how they
                  identify.
                  You made
                 a whole life.
                  Smoothed
           it out good.   Babies to
             love their   mothers
             & fathers.   Were you
            happy for   them when
           they got up   & out? Yes,
           we can call   it a con, yet
           everyone's   been more
          or less afloat.   Moreso than
          the average in   that apartment
          house. You   hardly see them.
          I see them   more. Where I
          eat, where I   do marvels in
         all those un   sung places.
         (Here they   are. & they
        all say no.)   I don't mean
        those. I mean   the others.
       (No other   children?) I
      didn't have.   many. That's
      the real one   who came
      with pie. You   don't really
     need it, unless   you lack. He
    doesn't know you, but he
      loves the idea of you.

             "My children
           are untended.
          Out of my
         reach. Un
        tended by
       our own."   Grandma
      on the   psychic
     hi fi. Yet   the de
    signated   caretakers
   think much   of invisible
  guides &   spurs, & isn't
 that tend   ing? More
than visiting   what's pre
sumed left of   them since
 dates (they   don't own)
 were set in   rock over
  those re   m(a)inders.
 They didn't   ask for that
 future meet   ing; I didn't
 mention. A   long car
schlep to gain   sense-drain
 ed metonymy. Before the
 decade expires, we can con
  vert video tapes to DVD.

HOME COOKED DIAMOND 15

                    My mother
                    will take
                    care of
                    you. No
                    rickety
                    debit card   this round.
                    You'll pay up   big, big
                    man, till zero   remainder.
                    Free will: a   cute pup
                    dream. At   bottom,
                    genetically   imprinted,
                    you're glee   ful to be
                    lost, chronic   ally sheepish.
                    Where among   the current
                    graduates will   you spy
                    such aromatic   deep-dish
                    patriarchy as   in her com
                    petence, con   fidence—
                    insuperable?   (Stem-cell
                    analysis could   have fetch
                    ed her primal   joy.) & the
                    hardscrabble business grits
                    through another terri
                    fying recession.

The cat is
bigger than
the child.
Wailing kid?   Whaling
guardian. Na.   Maximum
insecurity frisson.   In retrospect,
your mother   started wear
ing pants in   the mid 60s.
Can progress   glide on this
liberation?   Were we
brought up   to fart in
front of   elders? Some
therapy   gets incontin
ent with   motif rep
etition. I'm   willing to
rejuvenate   the juvenilia,
but its crust   can be in
transigent,   misprision
impossible   to break out
of. Any sealant   radically changes
the colors. You're   my wire. Would
it were strong. One function of the
group photo is to comb out
conflict. The shut door's
enough of a primal scene.

At entry
a tender
virus trans   mits
zigzag land   marks,
order pro   portionate,
(perhaps   proper) to
ardor of   progenitors,
who are   becoming
live octopi   within Precious'
body. "If I   had a child there,
I'd want to   get them out."
Phantoms   to coat what
shivering   image rises
out & up.   Some extract
for you   there, extracted
from am   bition salt.
Tabula   not so rasa
calibrates   the mama's
hoops &   is c(l)ued
soon into   the paternal
gavel rap.   Some grow
estranged   from doubt;
those, moth   ered by thunder
storm, who depart from
chronic inscription slice
up, juggle worst, best,
between of legacy.

Where
did they
stuff his   rose?
The figures   behind
the iron   kiln door
care &   care to
blame—   correctively.
A toboggan   thunders
rashly down   to that
variant   claimed
to be   him. His
plastic   prize has
been   thought to
prove a   means to
secede   from ob
lique   terrors.
Does   it fail to
age?   Holds a
quest   ionable
warranty.   He aims to
restrain the   object's dis
persive properties, retrain
its skittery course, retain
baseline succor.

A
blood   pack
does not   enforce
a blood   pact. "I
have a   PhD in
Mom."   Pretext
for a   lamp to
probe,   a lamb
to scratch.   "To visit
her im   mediately."
But can't   such crises
be self-   medicated?
Embrace   & assault:
toward   realization
of what   she presumes
is the   happiest denoue
ment. The   holiday is never
less than   succulent, as you
came to anti   cipate items
close to memory's start. What
tummy can stay bitter?
What mouth?

.

NOTES AND ACKNOWLEDGMENTS

Grateful acknowledgment is made to the following publications where poems appeared, sometimes in different versions:

Barrow Street: "Yinglish Strophes 22 & 23"

BlazeVox: "Dusk Bowl Intimacies 32 & 33"; "Home Cooked Diamond 1 & 2"; Previous version of "Home Cooked Diamond 2," formerly called "Artless Condo on an Exhausted Cliff," also published in Peace Conference (Marsh Hawk Press, 2011)

Blue and Yellow Dog: "Dented Reprise 11"; "Home Cooked Diamond 11 & 12"; "Jigsaw Hubbub 5 & 6, 16 & 17"

Coconut: "Home Cooked Diamond 14, 15, & 16"

Cricket Online Review: "Dusk Bowl Intimacies 22, 23, & 24"

Diode: "Dented Reprise 12 & 13"; "Jigsaw Hubbub 7 & 8"

E-ratio: "Dusk Bowl Intimacies 36 & 37"

In Transit: "Syllabus"

Locus Point: "Burgh's Bloom (Hay[na]ku/Box)"; "Goad 26"; "Jigsaw Hubbub 11 & 12"; "Yinglish Strophes 24"

Marsh Hawk Review: "Dusk Bowl Intimacies 25"; "Jigsaw Hubbub 13 & 14"

Milk: "Dusk Bowl Intimacies 34 & 35"; "Jigsaw Hubbub 9 & 10"

Moria: "Hay(na)ku Exfoliation 12, 13, & 14"

Of(f)course: "As We Repeat (Deconstricted Sestina)"; "Dusk Bowl Intimacies 26, 27, & 28"

Otoliths: "All the Tennis in Tennessee"; "Home Cooked Diamond 4 & 5"; "How Much Money Do I"; "Odd Ditties, Tar Errata"

Press 1: "Goad 20 & 21"

Raft: "Jigsaw Hubbub 3 & 4"

Spiral Orb: "Goad 17"

Talisman: "Goad 18 & 19"; "Home Cooked Diamond 10" (previous version, formerly called "Dangerous Intersection," also published in *Clarity and Other Poems* [Marsh Hawk Press, 2008]); "Jigsaw Hubbub 1 & 2"

The term "Yinglish," coined by Leo J. Rosten, indicates Yiddish syntax imported into English.

In the "Dusk Bowl Intimacies" series, each poem can be considered a haibun, with a hay(na)ku or sequence of them at the end. The hay(na)ku is Eileen Tabios' invention, and she has labeled haibun followed by her form "haybun." In my version of this hybrid form, which I call haibu(na)ku, the paragraph must have an equal number of sentences as the hay(na)ku or chain of hay(na)ku has words.

Photo and painting of author: Maya Diablo Mason

THOMAS FINK, born in New York City in 1954, is the author of seven previous books of poetry, including *Peace Conference* (Marsh Hawk Press, 2011) and *Autopsy Turvy* (Meritage Press, 2010), a book of collaborative poetry with Maya Diablo Mason, as well as three chapbooks. He is also the author of two books of criticism, including *"A Different Sense of Power": Problems of Community in Late-Twentieth-Century U.S. Poetry* (Fairleigh Dickinson University Press, 2001). With Joseph Lease, he is co-editor of *"Burning Interiors": David Shapiro's Poetry and Poetics* (Fairleigh Dickinson University Press, 2007). His poem, "Yinglish Strophes IX," was selected for *The Best American Poetry 2007* (Scribner's) by Heather McHugh and David Lehman. Fink's work has appeared in *American Poetry Review, Barrow Street, Chicago Review, Contemporary Literature, Denver Quarterly, Diode, Jacket, Lit, Milk, Minnesota Review, Otoliths, Second Avenue Poetry, Sentence, Shampoo, Slope, Talisman, Verse,* and numerous other journals. His paintings hang in various collections. Fink is Professor of English at City University of New York—LaGuardia.

Titles From Marsh Hawk Press

For more information, please go to: http://www.marshhawkpress.org.